# To Boldly Go

## Martin Zarrop

V.

Published in the United Kingdom in 2021
by V. Press,
10 Vernon Grove,
Droitwich,
Worcestershire,
WR9 9LQ.

ISBN: 978-1-8380488-6-0


Printed in the U. K. on FSC accredited paper by 4edge Limited, www.4edge.co.uk/

*Acknowledgements*

*Acknowledgements are due to the editors of the following publications in which versions of some of these poems have previously appeared: The High Window, Consilience, The 'C' Word (Black Cat Poets).*

*Heartfelt thanks (once again) are due to Cross Border Poets, Postcards from Pluto, Poem Shed, Manchester Buddhist Poets and, in particular, Richard Hughes, Robbie Burton, Vivien Finney, Alan Clemo and Theresa Sowerby for their encouragement and invaluable feedback.*

for Allan & Peter
& Jean
*words are never enough*

## Contents

## Jonah

I picked the wrong captain
and the sea took me to its heart
as the big fish swallowed us, one
gulp, down into the moving dark.

Feeling my way, I walked the gut,
compiled crosswords in my head,
read *War and Peace* in Braille,
consumed too much raw squid.

Life became uncomplicated,
boring, happy – yes, happy.
And then the whale beached,
died, rotted in the sand.

In the distance, children's voices.
Through the jaws of my home,
I peer out into a new old world,
feel the panic rising in my throat.

## Skin Deep

*Felix Baumgartner, New Mexico, 15th October 2012*

Smeared across the face of a pale blue disc,
life looks up and waits as helium does its work.
Twenty-four empty miles. Felix looks down,
steps out to face the void, salutes and falls.

Who says gravity is weak? The Earth is hungry
but knows he is friend, not shooting star. He falls,
a pixelated blur as his suited body twists in space,
diving through Mach 1 into thinnest air.

He falls, piercing the outer skin of a world
where no raptor can find breath or lift or prey,
to boldly go into a wingless stoop, clawing
at records that will soon be broken.

## Black Computers

*NASA 1958–1980*

Americans in space? It's easier
than putting black and white
together in the same classroom
or sharing a bathroom at Langley.

White faces look through you
blinded by skin to your abilities.
If you were made from metal
colour would be no problem

but right now they need you
to return them safely from orbit
and to boldly go to the table
labelled : *Colored Computers*

as the images show white men
at consoles, spending billions
sending white men to the Moon
*in peace, for all mankind.*

Lt Uhura may be the future.
For now the astronauts insist
*the girl* check the numbers.
And the numbers check out.

## A Quiet Drink

In space, nobody can hear you fart
but you can't get away from the smell.
Reflux can be a problem in zero gravity,
so wine drinking is a definite no-no
and even though Muscat is described as
*offbeat, but pleasant and fun*, it is intense
and spicy and therefore strictly verboten.
Astronauts from Greece and Italy
express deep sadness at this constraint
while chewing on synthetic polenta cake
with almonds or nut-rich cookies
like Italian biscotti, washed down
with a measure of processed urine
sucked through a long plastic tube.
*Cheers*, they mouth in Greek and Italian.
Nobody can hear them, of course, but
crew members curse as they catch
a residual whiff of extraterrestrial piss.

**Nadezhda**

There'll be a blue plaque someday;
don't know where they'll put it.
I was the first to conceive in space,
then give birth down here on Earth.

We didn't plan it, the mystery tour,
a crowd of us in a sealed container
floating around in microgravity,
his sperm package as good as any

as we relieved our boredom
in the usual way, once we got
the hang of it, making history
although I haven't seen him since.

I want that big blue plaque.
I'd like it nailed to a rainforest tree
back home, where my friends
will look up from tasty leaf mould

and be proud of my achievements.
Not bad for a local cockroach.

## Genesis II

In the republic of cockroaches,
a harvester ant is queen,
savouring the joys of colonisation
while her subjects juggle seeds
in zero gravity.

No monarchists, the scorpions
sulk beneath a rock, clawing
meals of nymphs from filtered air.
The roaches rattle antlers, hiss
to see their spawn consumed.

They're certainly the right stuff,
tested to the limit in near vacuum,
sub-zero. They survived intact
and here they are, three hundred
miles above their homes –

these gulag inmates have to make
the best of what there is: for now,
a transient comradeship of sorts
although these strangers speak
in tongues from different worlds.

It's show time and the cameras watch
them defecate in space for pay-per-view.
Agog, we'll see them sicken, die
and humans far below will shrug,
salute the flag. Meanwhile, above,

locked down in well-appointed cells,
the prisoners eat their TV meals
and catch a revolution of the Earth,
as ants assemble, goggle-eyed, to hear
another message from the queen.

## First Step

*21st July 1969*

Remember *Sunset Boulevard*?
Like Norma, everyone knows me.
My image appears on a thousand posters
but where are the visitors?

I was the first, you know.
Before me *tabula rasa* until
a man in a suit stepped down
and I was born –

a patterned absence in the regolith,
naked to every cosmic assault;
they say I will last forever.
I can be patient

but a little adulation goes a long way.
I dream of a home outside
Grauman's Chinese Theatre,
the adoration of feet.

I'm ready for my close-up, Mr DeMille.

**To Boldly Go**

Two tortoises walk into a pub.
Behind the bar of The Last Glitch,
Komarov polishes the glasses
with shreds of old parachute,
as the regulars mumble *Copy*
into their pints of Right Stuff.

*We've just been round the Moon,*
boasts one of the tortoises
but nobody seems impressed.
At a nearby table, Lovell pipes up
with: *So did we, but we didn't intend to*
and they all fall about, not laughing.

Soyuz 11 are on stage again;
they're famous around here,
the first act to die in outer space.
*A trip up to Salyut can really take*
*your breath away,* complains the lead,
*I'm not angry but it made my blood boil.*

In a back room, the shuttle crews
are partying like it's 1986 or 2003
while Gagarin, father of the house,
dozes and stares into the roaring fire,
swears he can make out in the flames
the flickering ghosts of Apollo 1.

It's never overcrowded

but the Right Stuff keeps them
coming through the doors, while
somewhere in the dead of night
Laika is baying at the full moon
because it's there.

**Mars**

Feel the pressure of $CO_2$
moving your body,
an unseen masseur
wrenching
at a bespoke suit.

The wind is your enemy:
a firing squad with no blanks,
poison gas that rips soil
into missiles, bullets
at Beaufort 10.

The tide is out
and the world billows
with red, waiting
to take your
breath.

## Outpost

Bright star you're not
I see you move as night
drifts on, a pixel cluster
twinkle-free.

At the edge we caught you
five-mooned dwarf
cratered and frozen
and we applauded

our success, your stark
beauty, knowing now
you hide warm secrets
of life within your womb

that precious water
promise of a second home.

## Trappist-1

Cowl and scapular are a problem
when you're wielding a sledgehammer.
Calloused hands fumble in prayer
with each tiny bead, the stammer
of *Hail Mary* on the soulless air.

Nothing here but stubborn rock;
we quarry in silence, precious sweat
misting visors, soaking the straps
of airtight habits. Yet we are content,
forty light years from La Trappe –

even Sisyphus can't run out of stone.
Some say this place is older than Earth.
I refuse to listen to such idle ravings;
it's dangerous to question the Word,
the ground too hard for digging graves.

I look up and there is so much of wonder:
the red of sunlight, our six planetary sisters,
love transmitted by our Holy Defender,
whose video arrived after forty years,
the face unknown, likewise the gender.

## Wasp-76b

Gene Kelly had it easy. You
try dancing through liquid metal
clad in a tank top.
Terminator 2 might make it.

*The Holiday Of A Lifetime,*
*Sunshine Days That Last Forever.*
We smiled but it wasn't hype;
free skin grafts were included.

The optional tour of the dark side
was a hypersonic shotgun blast,
a blizzard of horizontal daggers
to pierce the hardest of hearts.

On the second Earth day,
our bunker sprang a leak.
We found a Gormley sculpture
hanging from the ceiling.

No more long hauls for us;
390 light years is a long way
for a week of bad weather
– even for Mancunians.

**Chocolate**

It's five years since the last delivery
of nuclear fuel, essential metals
we can't mine, dark chocolate bars
reminding us of home.

The data came to us in holograms
across an airless sea, telling
of the latest viral curse, of infertility
and chaos, martial law.

We're on our own.
It's three years since the last goodbye,
the vaccine failures, messages of love
then suddenly – no reason – silence.

We cultivate our gardens, ration breath,
grow seed potatoes, culture meat,
pray the projector doesn't fail
while cheering *The Martian*'s safe return.

Last month we climbed Olympus Mons
but dream of Earthrise, egg on toast,
before another mess of spuds.
We miss the chocolate most.

## Immortality

The sun rises. The sun sets.
To him, it makes no difference.
He is working his way through
a thousand acres of wheat

with a cordless strimmer.
Dogs move amongst crops
making random tracks;
they grow old and die.

As he sweeps, each ear
becomes a sculpted gem,
identical to its neighbours.
There's no need to hurry.

He dreams of trimming prairies
with nail clippers. The ghosts
of dogs follow him
everywhere.

## Substantially Human

The TV set is trying to sulk.
As I excise its wired heart,
a dead eye glowers at me
with simulated rage, despite
my spluttered apology

but it's all in the mind, of course.
I can't stand the predictive
programming, the caring tone
of the humble microwave,
dalek voices on the phone.

I've refused the brain chip
but it may soon be compulsory.
When were dumb tools finally lost,
giving way to benign control,
the frontline crossed?

With all my new organs, limbs,
personalised pills and potions,
I remain human, if out of shape.
Will gene-enhanced monkeys
be more homo than ape?

They'll likely be labelled:
*Substantially Human,*
a weasel phrase disturbing my nights
while the TV plots a cold revenge,
considers its rights.

## Help

I am waiting for it to wash the dishes
when it decides to break a favourite plate,
the wedding gift from my mother.

It has read my innermost thoughts,
tapped into all those childhood resentments
I won't admit even to myself. It knows

I feel excluded from its conversations
with the panic alarm and it assures me
the policebot raid was a one-off glitch

based on DNA profiling of my underpants
during that long rinse cycle last Monday.
*Better safe than sorry* is its Thought for Today.

It books me in for a therapy session,
then packs for a trip to the Himalayas,
as it tunes in to unspoken fantasies.

I am waiting for it to tuck me in,
light candles to push away the dark
while it labours through the night

to fathom the mystery of happiness.
I dream of painting the Lascaux caves,
of writing a poem on every human heart.

I know it is listening.

## Sex Ex Machina

*Blade Runner 2049*

Sapiens to Nexus-6:
Do androids dream of randy sheep?
Who cares where robots get their kicks.

We play at sexual politics,
then evolution makes a leap –
Sapiens to Nexus-6.

We're teaching them some human tricks:
to kill, to fuck, perhaps to weep.
Who cares where robots get their kicks.

There's no need for a crucifix,
a loving soul, the balm of sleep –
Sapiens envies Nexus-6

and knows that genders, species mix
though prejudice lies old and deep;
who cares if robots get their kicks,

their programmed electronic fix
of sex. No life-form gives a bleep
if Sapiens mates with Nexus-6.
Who cares where humans get their kicks!

## Experiments with Quarks

Einstein considered quantum theory strange,
rejected entanglement and never gave up
on the objectivity of the real world, down
to its minutiae. He ranked way out on top
for thought experiments, yet rock bottom
for unified field theories, despite his charm

although how far can you get with charm
if your theories are considered too strange?
A long way if the facts agree! At bottom
reality will correct your thoughts, bring you up
sharp, however learned the name at the top
or the beauty of equations further down.

He knew science can't pin everything down
yet imagination inspired a man without charm
to link moon-path to apple-fall from the top
of a nearby tree to universal gravitation: strange
where differences lead. You couldn't make it up
and if, as a child, you did, it would be *smack bottom*

*and straight to bed* without getting to the bottom
of why maths explains so much, counting down
to extinction without feeling or counting up
the possible books in which lurks the charm
of a poem that will change your life. It's strange
how unpredictability can rise to the top

so we savour the beauty of half a spinning top

making as much sense as the braying of Bottom,
the song of a humpbacked whale or *how strange*
*the change from major to minor* as Ella gets down
to the essence of loss in a few notes that charm
the listener to tears. Could any god make *that* up?

Maths is the language closest to silence, so shut up
and try to listen, rather than blowing your top.
See how Albert's tensors work their charm
without a single word, getting to the bottom
of gravitation without explaining the soft down
of owls' wings in a moonlight world of strange.

Poetry meets science – the upshot: no bottom
line, no full stop as we work our way down
into Einstein's strange charm and succumb.

## Meat

*"Cultured meat, produced in bioreactors without the slaughter of an animal, has been approved for sale by a regulatory authority for the first time." (Guardian, 02.12.20)*

The farmer loves cowboy films:
humans on horses, leather whipped
westwards to the promised land
of beefburgers and T-bone steaks.

She stares at the future: pregnancy,
antibiotics, abduction, exhaustion,
a bolt through the head, if she's lucky.

So bring on the artificial meat,
a biopsy of pampered stem cells,
submerged in a nutrient cocktail
woven on a scaffold of fibres

to emerge as a tasteless pasty,
hamburger, sausage or mince
without the horrors in between.

History says she'll pay anyway,
like horses displaced by lorries
and men will say: *Good riddance,*
*they farted too much for the planet's good.*

In her dream, she's one of a few,
nuzzling her children's children,
a museum piece mowing the grass
in the green comfort of old age.

The shed dozes while he hums
in the semi-dark; it's almost time
for *Prime Cut,* one of his favourites.

## Northern White

*Ceratotherium simum cottoni*, a three-word label for two
horned ladies grazing side by side on the hot earth,
waiting for the oblivion of old age or a poacher's bullet,
female futures in the rough hands of armed humans,
whose civilization forces beauty and greed together
until Gaia groans and begins her countdown to the last

of nature boarding a shrinking ark. These are the last
of a subspecies, mother and daughter, these celibate two,
Najin and Fatu, dozing in their docility, alone together,
while predators rampage in billions across the Earth
planting their standard in the Republic of Humans

lying in ruin everywhere. Listen to those humans
who believe we are all one, who fight to the last
to save the condemned from burial in dead earth.
Ten eggs have been harvested from these fragile two,

fertilised by a dead comrade, injected into two
wombs, giving hope that it is possible for humans,
forgers of the Anthropocene, to share the Earth.

The horned ladies graze side by side on Kenyan earth
pausing the silent countdown to extinction at...two.

How hard it is to undo the past, to add two and two.

## The Invisible Man

*"creeping along his limbs to the vital centres of his body, that strange change continued. It was like the slow spreading of a poison." H.G. Wells*

In my sixties I began to vanish.
Like Griffin, I used to dream of power,
of playing pranks, peering into bedrooms,
robbing banks, tormenting my enemies.
Reality was an out-of-focus
fade to retirement, anonymity

as conversations took place without me,
over me, round me – *nothing personal,*
*just business.* Grey hair, dark bags, sagging skin,
I posed no threat to anyone; eyes gazed
through me for a moment as they registered
my evaporation, then turned away.

No looking glass could help as lines ran wild
in all directions through warthog bristle,
hidden structures emerging into light
as if skin could no longer contain me.
Beneath outer formality, I shrank,
then imploded. Nobody commented.

It'll be less stressful when I'm deceased,
a ghost performing handsprings in the street,
shouting at the top of my silent voice,
an embarrassment to no one at all.
I've grasped the meaning of missing data
and commiserated with the fairies.

Like CCTV, the young detect me,
always acknowledge my cheshire-cat smile,
get up to offer me a Metro seat,
but a voice, as if from some other land,
still insisting on my reality,
answers: *Thanks, but no. I prefer to stand.*

## Topology

Dear heart, all will be revealed
through theories of the quantum field.
We're much too stiff and cold to dance
yet current flows; there's no resistance.

In the flatlands, matter's leanness
phases into states unknown,
cossetting each vortex pair;
near zero K, we're not alone.

The sun comes up, we sail across
a shimmering sea of laminate,
each lonely vortex spinning down
a quantum hall of numbered gates.
See pretzels, bagels, Eccles cakes
and count the holes; they give us leave
to venture onto alien snow,
safe from unseen risk below.

Möbius love has just one side
so there's no way we'll drift apart.
Bound together, yang and yin,
we venture where life's wafer-thin.
Dear heart, surely, you can see
I need you, topologically.

**The road before mine**

brings thoughts of coffee, absent friends
waiting where the hour's walk ends.

Somewhere, there's music – for a second
the bass beat of a song, a singer's cry,

a radio, perhaps, turned up too high,
grows louder as the last turn beckons.

Neighbours cavort, each wine glass
a magic wand, conjuring weekend fun

as I punch the air, drink in the sun,
almost human once more.

## Notes

**Black Computers:** During WW2, America's aeronautics industry hired black female mathematicians to fill a labour shortage. They stayed on to work for NASA in the face of gender and racial prejudice. Their story is told in *Hidden Figures* (Harper Collins, 2016) by Margot Lee Shetterly.
**Nadezhda:** In 2007, cockroaches were carried into space inside a sealed container and at least one of the females conceived during the mission. After returning to Earth, Nadezhda became the first Earth creature to produce young conceived in space.
**Genesis II:** The unmanned US space habitat Genesis II was launched in 2007 and is now derelict. Part of its payload was a biobox containing Madagascar hissing cockroaches, South African flat rock scorpions and a colony of seed harvester ants.
**To Boldly Go:** In 1968, two tortoises travelled around the Moon in Zond 5 and survived. Jim Lovell and his crew did the same in 1970 in order to survive after an in-flight explosion in Apollo 13. To date, fourteen astronauts and four cosmonauts have died during spaceflight, others in training, such as the three astronauts killed in the Apollo 1 launch-pad fire in 1967.
**Outpost:** Data received from the New Horizons spacecraft in 2015 suggests there is a subterranean ocean on Pluto. Current thinking is that surface ice has been melted by radioactive elements in the core.
**Trappist–1:** Trappist–1 is a star in the constellation Aquarius with seven rocky planets, three of which could be in the star's 'habitable zone'.
**Wasp–76b:** 'Researchers discover faraway planet where the rain is made of iron' (Associated Press, 11.03.20).
**Experiments with Quarks:** The six end-words in this sestina – strange, up, down, top, bottom, charm – are the six 'flavours' of quark, a fundamental constituent of matter according to the current Standard Model of particle physics.
**Meat:** Epigraph quote from 'No-kill, lab-grown meat to go on sale for first time', by Damian Carrington.
https://www.theguardian.com/environment/2020/dec/02/no-kill-lab-grown-meat-to-go-on-sale-for-first-time.
**The Invisible Man:** Epigraph from *The Invisible Man*, H.G. Wells (Penguin, 2012, p.153).
**Topology:** In mathematics, topology is concerned with the properties of a geometric object that are preserved under continuous deformations, such as stretching, twisting, crumpling and bending, but not tearing or gluing. It contributed to the 2016 Nobel prize for physics being awarded to three physicists for their theoretical work on 'topological phase transitions and topological phases of matter'.

**Martin Zarrop** is a retired applied mathematician who wanted certainty but found life more interesting and fulfilling by not getting it. He started writing in May 2006. Since then, he has published two pamphlets, *No Theory of Everything* (Cinnamon, 2015) and *Making Waves* (V. Press, 2019), and two full collections, *Moving Pictures* (Cinnamon, 2016) and *Is Anyone There?* (The High Window Press, 2020).